STEM
STORIES

Automobiles

FROM HENRY FORD TO ELON MUSK

Kelly Doudna

Checkerboard
Library

An Imprint of Abdo Publishing
abdopublishing.com

ABDOPUBLISHING.COM

Printed in the United States of America, North Mankato, Minnesota
052018
092018

THIS BOOK CONTAINS
RECYCLED MATERIALS

Design and production: Mighty Media, Inc.
Editor: Liz Salzmann
Cover Photographs: Library of Congress (left), Shutterstock (middle, right)
Interior Photographs: AP Images, pp. 21, 27, 28–29 (bottom); iStockphoto, pp. 4–5, 22, 25, 29 (top); Joe deSousa/Wikimedia Commons, pp. 7, 28 (top); Library of Congress, p. 13; National Archives and Records Administration, p. 15; Shutterstock, pp. 9, 11, 19, 23, 28 (bottom); sv1ambo/Flickr, p. 17

Library of Congress Control Number: 2017961637

Publisher's Cataloging-in-Publication Data
Name: Doudna, Kelly, author.
Title: Automobiles: From Henry Ford to Elon Musk / by Kelly Doudna.
Other titles: From Henry Ford to Elon Musk
Description: Minneapolis, Minnesota : Abdo Publishing, 2019. | Series: STEM stories |
      Includes online resources and index.
Identifiers: ISBN 9781532115448 (lib.bdg.) | ISBN 9781532156168 (ebook)
Subjects: LCSH: Automobiles--History--Juvenile literature. | Automobile industry and
      trade--History--Juvenile literature. | Inventors--Biography--Juvenile literature.
Classification: DDC 629.222092--dc23

Contents

The Road Most Traveled

Are you looking forward to getting your driver's license? Do you dream about the kind of car you want to own someday? Maybe you want to design and build the cars of the future!

Throughout history, people have desired to travel the world. First there were carts and wagons pulled by animals. Then came steam-powered trains. But the automobile changed travel forever.

Cars let people travel quickly nearly anywhere they wanted to go. People no longer had to depend on train schedules or follow train tracks. Eventually, anyone could learn to drive a car and most people could afford to own one.

In 2016, 17.5 million cars were sold in the United States. This was more cars than any other year before!

Automobile development started in the 1400s. But cars would not be practical until the late 1800s and early 1900s. That is when Henry Ford and others made important advancements. Improvements have continued to the present day, thanks to the automobile industry and **entrepreneurs** such as Elon Musk.

Cars have never been safer and easier to operate than they are now. And self-driving cars are just around the corner. Who knows where automobile **technology** will take us next?

CHAPTER 1

Early Ideas

The history of the automobile goes back hundreds of years. In the 1400s, artist Leonardo da Vinci sketched a design for a self-**propelled** vehicle. Starting in the 1700s, inventors explored different ways to make vehicles move. There were designs for steam, electric, and gasoline engines.

In 1769, French engineer Nicolas-Joseph Cugnot constructed the first true automobile. His machine was huge and heavy and had three wheels. It was propelled by steam. Cugnot's 1769 model could go 2.25 miles per hour (3.6 kmh) and carry four people. It was a military vehicle designed to haul weapons such as cannons.

Early steam engines were slow and required heavy equipment. Inventors in England, Germany, France, and the United States pursued design improvements. Steam-driven vehicles continued to be popular until the early 1900s.

Parts and methods created by several inventors were later combined in automobile design. In the 1600s, German engineer Otto von Guericke invented **pistons** and **cylinders**. Around the

Cugnot's vehicle was very heavy due to a large steam engine and boiler. The vehicle had to stop every ten minutes to build up steam.

same time, Dutch scientist Christiaan Huygens built an engine that used air pressure from a controlled explosion. In 1801, French engineer Philippe Lebon made a plan for a motor with an electric fuel pump and spark **ignition**. These would all be important elements of the **internal combustion engine**.

CHAPTER 2

Engine Improvements

Steam engines were abandoned in favor of gasoline engines in the early 1900s. This change was largely due to the development of the gasoline-powered **internal combustion engine**. Two of the first to use this type of engine were German engineers Gottlieb Daimler and Karl Benz. Daimler believed fitting carriages with engines was the way forward. However, Benz saw the car as a completely different vehicle from the beginning.

Though Benz and Daimler never met, they each built cars in the 1880s. Benz's had three wheels and was successfully driven around a test track in 1885. In 1886, Daimler modified a horse carriage to be **propelled** by an engine. Both men focused on patenting designs for engines. They then earned money licensing those patents to others.

Two French **innovators** who licensed Daimler's patent were René

FUN FACT

The oldest car still in running order is believed to be a Danish Hammel. It is in the Danish Museum of Science and Technology. It was built in 1888!

Panhard and Émile Levassor. They worked together to produce their first car in 1891. Also that year, Levassor was the first engineer to put the engine in the front of the car rather than in the rear. Levassor and Panhard also designed the transmission gear arrangement that became standard in all automobiles.

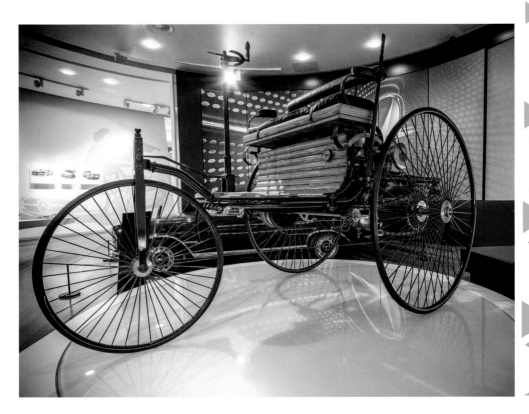

Benz's first car was called the Motorwagen. The car was first driven on a long trip by Benz's wife, Bertha. She drove it for 66 miles (106 km).

CHAPTER 3

American Ingenuity

Cars weren't only being built in Europe. The United States had its own automobile **innovators**. Brothers Charles E. Duryea and J. Frank Duryea were bicycle makers in Massachusetts. They turned their attention to cars and built a gas-powered model in 1893. By 1896, they had manufactured and sold 13 cars. These were the first sales of American-made, gasoline-powered automobiles.

The manufacture of cars caught on quickly. In 1897, Ransom E. Olds founded Oldsmobile in Michigan. In 1901, the company's Curved Dash Runabout model became the first mass-produced car with a total of 425 cars produced that year. In 1902, production jumped to 2,500 cars. In 1903, Oldsmobile produced 4,000 cars.

FUN FACT

In addition to the Duryeas, two other bicycle-making brothers were important American inventors. In 1903, Orville and Wilbur Wright designed and successfully flew the first airplane!

Olds was an early leader in car manufacturing. He was the first to use an assembly line. This kept the production costs low. Low production costs meant cars cost less for buyers. The Curved Dash sold for just $650. This low price meant owning a car was no longer a luxury reserved for the rich.

However, no one affected the automobile industry as much as Henry Ford. Ford wasn't the first to build cars or use an assembly line. But his **innovations** to both of these processes sparked the creation of today's automobile industry.

In 1901, a fire started at the Oldsmobile factory. The only car that survived the fire was the Oldsmobile Curved Dash.

CHAPTER 4

Supply and Demand

Ford Motor Company was founded in Michigan in 1903. In 1908, Ford released the first Model T. It was priced at $850. Between 1908 and 1927, Ford made more than 15 million Model Ts. By the time the last one rolled off the assembly line in 1927, its price had dropped to $290. The low cost made the car affordable for even more people.

By the 1930s, owning a car had become commonplace. Enough people had cars that demand for new vehicles leveled off. The **Great Depression** also contributed to the lower demand. People couldn't afford new cars. Then during **World War II**, car factories were converted to produce items for the military. New cars weren't **available**.

People nursed their old cars through the economic crisis and wartime shortage. When the war ended in 1945, owners were ready to buy new cars. The cars being made at the time were larger and more reliable. Consumers of the 1950s loved these modern automobiles!

Henry Ford

BORN: July 30, 1863, Dearborn, Michigan

DIED: April 7, 1947, Dearborn, Michigan

FACT: Ford designed his first car in 1896. It was a buggy with an engine. Ford called it the Quadricycle.

FACT: After production of the Model T ended, Ford produced the Model A. Nearly 5 million Model As were made between 1927 and 1931.

ACHIEVEMENTS

▶ Ford built a race car in 1902. He named it the 999 after the fastest train engine of the time.

▶ In 1914, Ford set the standard for manufacturing wages by paying his workers five dollars per eight-hour day.

▶ Ford used **vertical integration** at his factory in River Rouge, Michigan. He purchased coal and iron mines to produce materials needed to run the factory. And he used his own railroad and shipping companies to transport everything. Ford controlled the supply chain from start to finish.

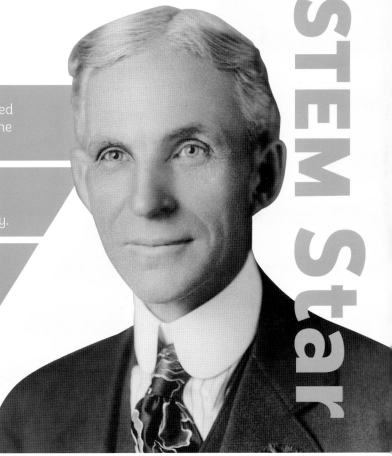

STEM Star

CHAPTER 5

Cars, Politics, and Oil

American automakers continued to design bigger, heavier cars throughout the 1950s and 1960s. These cars were faster and more comfortable than earlier models. They also used more gasoline. However, gas was inexpensive, so people didn't see this as a problem.

But in the early 1970s, gas prices rose. This is because the US was producing less oil, which is what gas is made from. The US had to import more oil from other countries.

Most of the oil the US purchased came from the Organization of Petroleum Exporting Countries (OPEC). OPEC is a group of nations in the Middle East. In October 1973, OPEC used its oil as a political weapon.

Many of the OPEC countries considered Israel to be their enemy. OPEC wanted to punish the US and other countries who supported Israel. So, OPEC reduced its oil production and raised prices. Within months, OPEC was charging almost four times the previous price for its oil.

During the oil crisis, the lines of cars at gas stations often extended for blocks. Many people had to wait in line for hours to buy gas.

As oil became more expensive, the cost of gas made from the oil also rose. This caused an energy crisis in the US that changed Americans' consumption habits. There was little gas **available** and it was suddenly very expensive. People no longer wanted large American cars that used a lot of gas. Buyers started purchasing smaller, imported cars that needed less gas than American cars.

The energy crisis wasn't the only event that sparked changes in the US auto industry. In the 1960s and 1970s, the US government imposed regulations in three main areas. The first area was safety. In 1966, federal safety standards came into effect. The requirements included seatbelts and padded interiors.

The second area that was regulated was car **emissions**. Car exhaust includes pollutants that damage the **environment**. In 1965, the government started requiring car makers to lower the amount of pollutants in the exhaust.

This effort was helped by the introduction of the catalytic converter in 1975. This device removes harmful chemicals from car exhaust. The catalytic converter had been invented by French engineer Eugene Houdry.

The third regulated area was fuel efficiency. Fuel efficiency is how far a car can travel on one gallon of gasoline. Due to the energy crisis, higher fuel-efficiency standards were set in 1975. The goal was to reduce gas consumption.

Due to these regulations and the public's demand for fuel-efficient cars, American companies started making compact cars. At the time, cars imported from Japan already met or exceeded American fuel-efficiency standards. These vehicles were also less expensive than American-made compact cars. US drivers embraced models such as the Toyota Corolla and Honda Civic, making them best-sellers.

The Volkswagen Beetle was a very popular compact car in the 1960s. It is one of the oldest model names still used today.

CHAPTER 6

Hybrids and EVs

While fuel-efficient cars remained popular, people kept looking for ways to further reduce gasoline use. One possibility was using electricity. Electric engines had been explored by some early automobile inventors.

These included English inventor Thomas Parker, German inventor Andreas Flocken, and Scottish-American inventor William Morrison. But electric cars couldn't compete with the travel range of gas-powered cars.

The turning point for electric cars came with hybrid cars. A hybrid uses both battery power and gasoline. When the battery's charge runs out, gasoline takes over powering the engine. The battery self-charges so the owner doesn't have to plug it in.

The first two hybrids **available** in the US were the Japanese-made Honda Insight and Toyota Prius. They were introduced in the US in 1999 and 2000. Ford became the first US automaker to produce a hybrid with the 2004 Escape SUV.

The Toyota Prius is the best-selling hybrid in the world. *Prius* is Latin for "to go before."

To encourage people to buy hybrids, federal and state governments offered benefits to hybrid drivers. These benefits included tax breaks and unlimited use of commuter lanes. Gas-electric hybrids had the power and the travel range to be commercially successful. By 2017, Toyota alone had sold more than 10 million hybrid cars.

Another turning point for electric cars came in 2008. That's when American auto company Tesla Motors started selling the Tesla Roadster. The Roadster could travel farther than 200 miles (322 km) on one charge. It was the first fully electric vehicle (EV) with this capability. However, the car was expensive, costing $100,000. Over three years, Tesla sold 2,250 Roadsters.

American businessman Elon Musk funded and oversaw the Roadster's development. He had joined Tesla's board in 2004. He later became the CEO and is now the face of the company. In 2017, the company name changed to Tesla, Inc.

Soon, other automakers developed their own EVs. The Nissan LEAF was released in 2010. The LEAF could travel 100 miles (160 km) on one charge. It cost about $30,000, so middle-class car buyers could afford it.

Tesla released the Model S in 2012. The Model S had a range of 265 miles (426 km) per charge. Tesla also installed Supercharger stations around the US and Europe. Drivers could charge their cars at these stations during long trips.

By 2018, most major car companies were offering electric and hybrid cars. There were more than 40 models **available**. Buyers could choose from a number of sizes and styles.

Elon Musk

BORN: June 28, 1971, Pretoria, South Africa

FACT: Musk's father is South African and his mother is Canadian. Musk is a citizen of those countries as well as the US.

FACT: Musk graduated from the University of Pennsylvania.

FACT: Musk wants to build a human colony on Mars.

ACHIEVEMENTS

▶ In 2002, Musk co-founded SpaceX, which makes rocket launchers and spacecraft. SpaceX has reduced the cost of manufacturing rockets and launching them into space. NASA has a rocket-launch contract with SpaceX.

▶ Musk didn't found Tesla Motors, but he joined the board as its chairman in 2004. He became CEO in 2008.

▶ In 2015, Musk founded OpenAI, a research company working toward development of safe artificial intelligence.

STEM Star

Automobiles:

PAST AND PRESENT

Early cars, such as the Ford Model T, have many of the same parts as modern cars, such as the Tesla Model 3. For example, they both have wheels, doors, headlights, and steering wheels. But many of these parts look very different in each car. And they each have parts the other doesn't.

FORD MODEL T

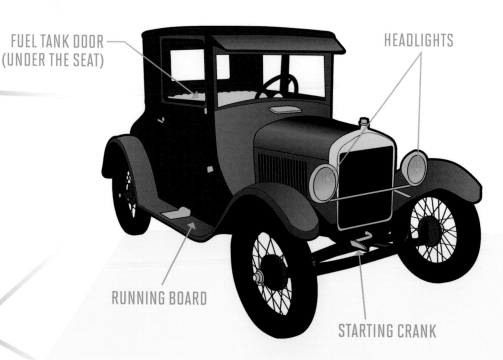

FUEL TANK DOOR
(UNDER THE SEAT)

HEADLIGHTS

RUNNING BOARD

STARTING CRANK

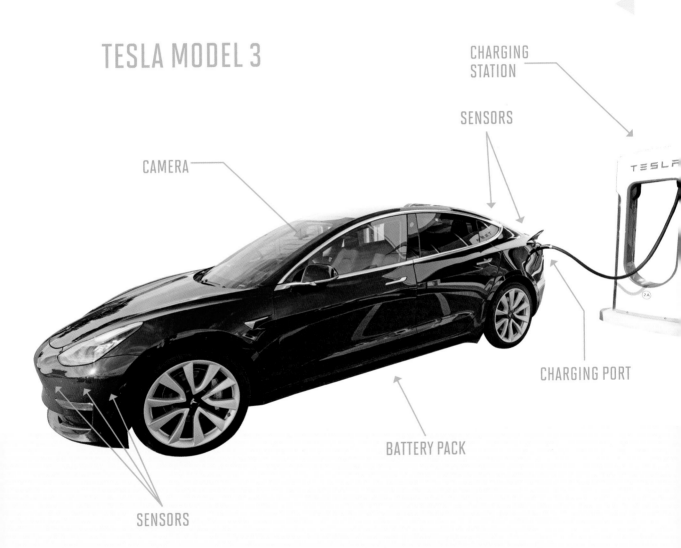

TESLA MODEL 3

CHARGING
STATION

SENSORS

CAMERA

CHARGING PORT

BATTERY PACK

SENSORS

CHAPTER 7

Fantastic Features

Engine mechanics and fuel efficiency aren't the only aspects of the automobile that have changed over time. Today's cars use computer **technology** in many ways. They can assist with driving, safety, and entertainment.

Cameras make backing up and parking easier. Some cars can even park on their own! The first car with self-parking technology was the 2003 Toyota Prius. Also, many cars now have built-in **GPS** devices that provide drivers with directions.

To improve safety, cars have **sensors** that alert drivers if they start to leave their lanes. Two of the first cars with this feature were the 2003 Honda Inspire and the 2005 Infiniti FX. Seats also have sensors that indicate whether they are occupied and turn on the air bags accordingly.

Entertainment systems in cars have also improved. Modern car entertainment systems can play music from smartphones and receive **satellite radio** signals. Passengers can watch movies on individual screens in the back seats.

Many features in a Tesla Model 3 are controlled by a large touchscreen on the dashboard. These features include the radio, heating, GPS, and more.

Dashboard computers can include owner's manuals, so people can learn about all of the car's fancy features. And owners don't have to worry about **software** updates. Those can be sent directly to the car's computer by the manufacturer.

CHAPTER 8

Autonomous Awesomeness

The modern car is edging closer to full autonomy. A car with full autonomy would be able to drive itself with no input from a human. Each new computer-controlled feature reduces the need for a human driver. Parallel parking assistance, lane-departure warnings, and **automatic** braking have become standard features.

Google began developing self-driving cars in 2009. In 2014, Tesla equipped its Model S with a self-driving function called Autopilot. Ride-sharing service Uber began its own tests of self-driving cars in 2015.

In 2016, Google formed the company Waymo to continue development of self-driving cars. Waymo began a public trial of self-driving minivans in Phoenix, Arizona, in 2017. It's possible that self-driving vehicles from Waymo and other companies will be **available** for ride-hailing in the next few years. Ride-hailing services include taxi companies, Uber, and Lyft.

When cars reach full autonomy, they will be able to interact with the users' smartphones. Cars will know who is riding in them

Waymo uses Chrysler Pacifica minivans for its autonomous cars.

and adjust interior features, such as temperature and music. Any controls still necessary inside the car might appear on a **hologram**-like display.

Fully autonomous cars will basically be computers with wheels. Passengers will be able to operate the vehicles using voice commands. Cars will no longer noisily spew pollutants from their tailpipes. Instead they will be electric, **emission**-free pieces of self-driving hardware!

Timeline

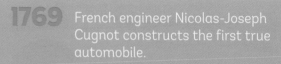

1769   French engineer Nicolas-Joseph Cugnot constructs the first true automobile.

1893   The Duryea brothers manufacture and sell the first American-made, gasoline-powered automobiles.

1901   The Oldsmobile Curved Dash Runabout becomes the first mass-produced car.

1908   Ford Motor Company releases the Model T.

1966   New US federal safety requirements include seatbelts and padded interiors.

1975 The catalytic converter is introduced as part of the exhaust system.

2004 Ford becomes the first US automaker to produce a gas-electric hybrid.

2008 Tesla Motors starts selling the all-electric Tesla Roadster.

2014 Tesla releases a Model S with a self-driving function called Autopilot.

2017 Waymo begins a public trial of self-driving minivans in Phoenix, Arizona.

Glossary

automatic—moving or acting by itself.

available—able to be had or used.

cylinder—a tube in which a piston of an engine moves.

emissions—substances released into the air, especially by smokestacks or automobiles.

entrepreneur—one who organizes, manages, and accepts the risks of a business or an enterprise.

environment—all the surroundings that affect the growth and well-being of a living thing.

GPS (Global Positioning System)—a space-based navigation system used to pinpoint locations on Earth.

Great Depression—the period from 1929 to 1942 of worldwide economic trouble. There was little buying or selling, and many people could not find work.

hologram—a three-dimensional picture made of light.

ignition—the device that is used to start a car's engine.

innovation—a new idea, method, or device. Someone who creates innovations is an innovator.

internal combustion engine—an engine in which the fuel is burned within engine cylinders.

piston—a cylinder fit inside a hollow cylinder in which it moves back and forth. It is moved by fluid pressure in an engine.

propel—to drive forward or onward by some force.

satellite radio—radio stations whose signals are transmitted by satellites in space.

sensor—an instrument that can detect, measure, and transmit information to a controlling device.

software—the written programs used to operate a computer.

technology (tehk-NAH-luh-jee)—machinery and equipment developed for practical purposes using scientific principles and engineering.

vertical integration—having control over the production and distribution steps needed to manufacture and sell a product.

World War II—from 1939 to 1945, fought in Europe, Asia, and Africa. Great Britain, France, the United States, the Soviet Union, and their allies were on one side. Germany, Italy, Japan, and their allies were on the other side.

Online Resources

Booklinks
NONFICTION NETWORK
FREE! ONLINE NONFICTION RESOURCES

To learn more about automobiles, visit **abdobooklinks.com**. These links are routinely monitored and updated to provide the most current information available.

Index